This book belongs to

_____

This book is dedicated to my children - Mikey, Kobe, and Jojo.

Copyright © Grow Grit Press LLC. All rights reserved. No part of this book may be reproduced in any form without permission in writing from the publisher. Please send bulk order requests to growgritpress@gmail.com 978-1-63731-298-8 Printed and bound in the USA. NinjaLifeHacks.tv

Ninja Life Hacks™

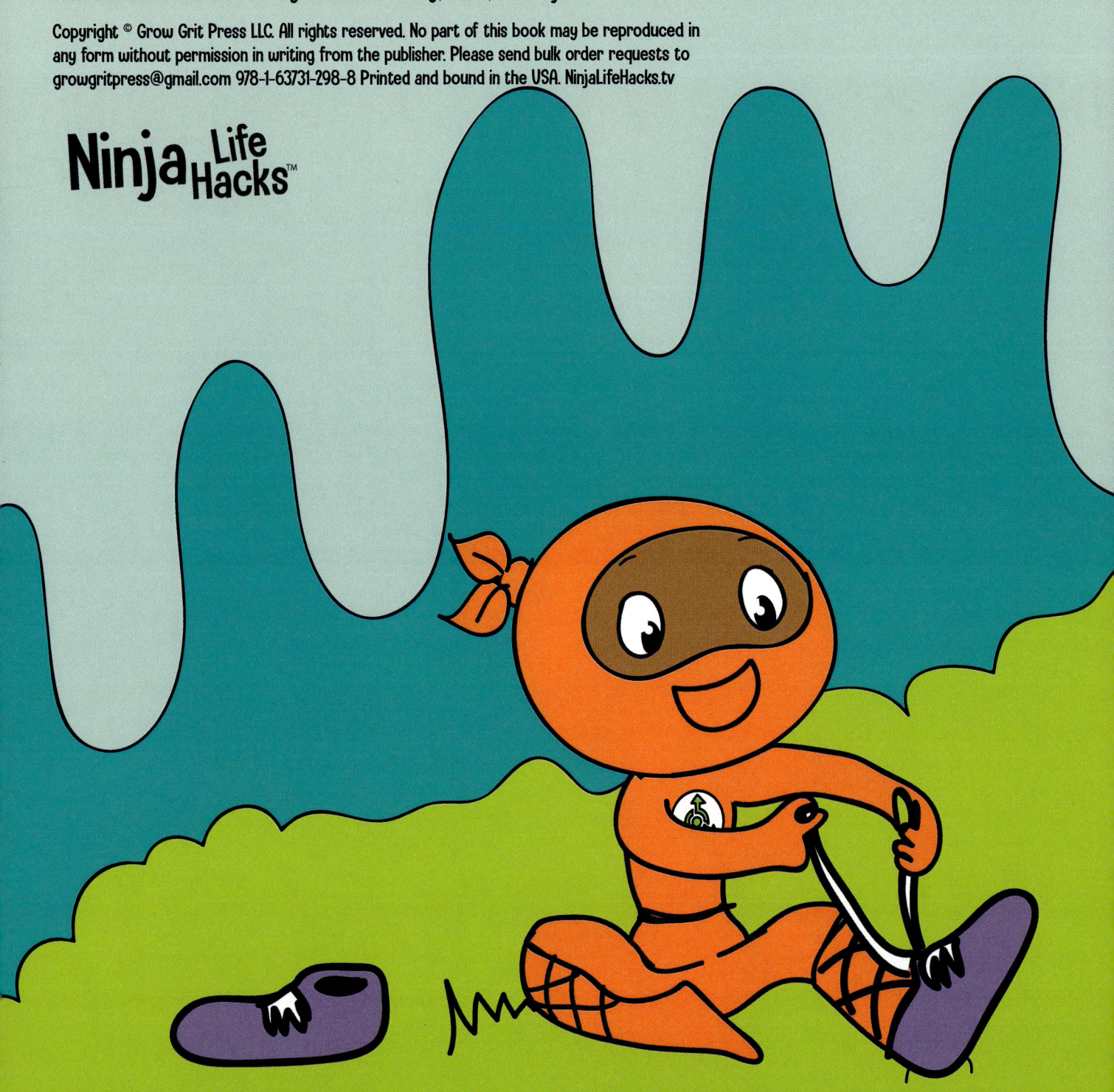

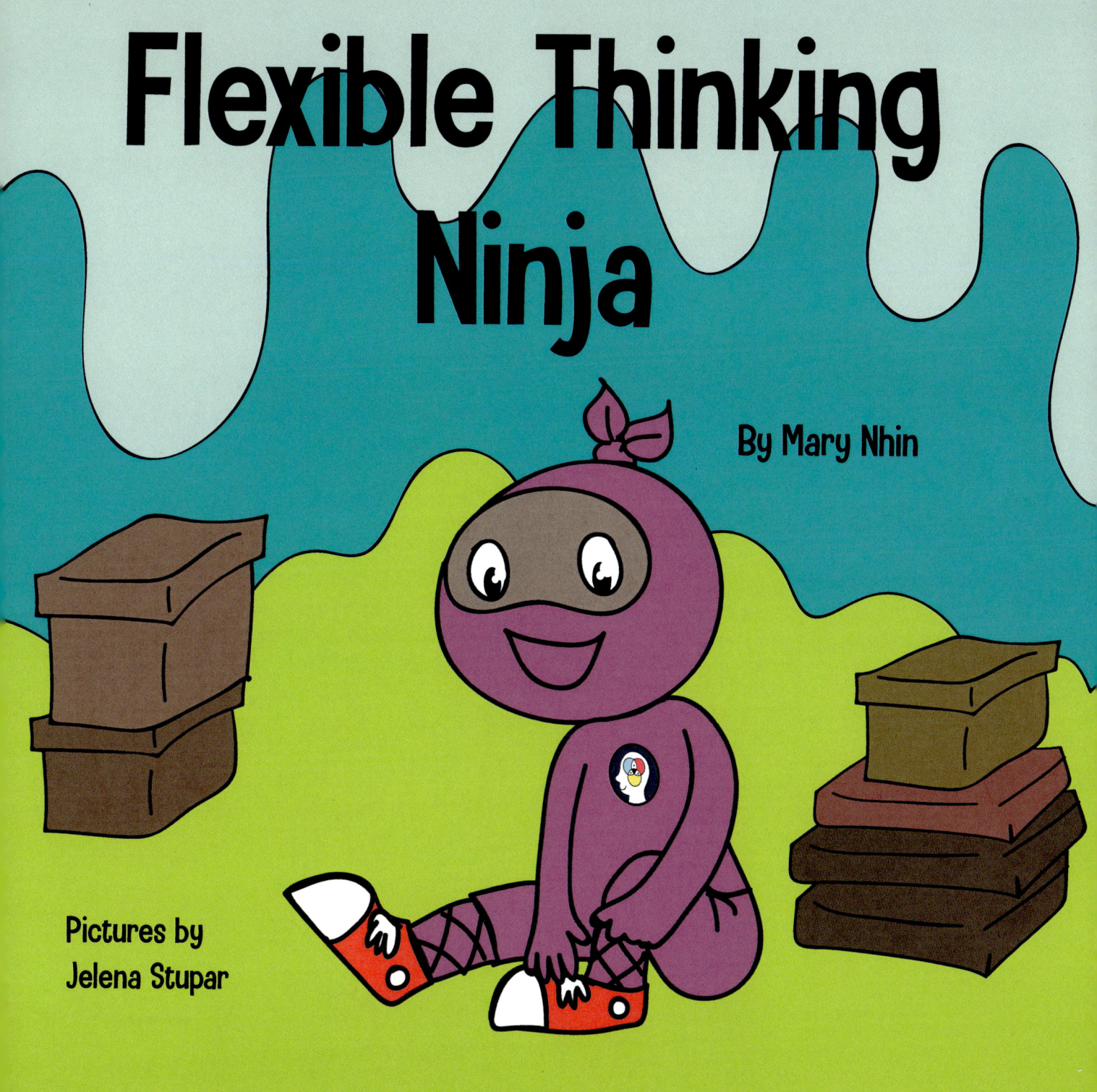

Hi! I'm Flexible Thinking Ninja.

I use my flexible thinking skills to problem solve, be creative, and look at a problem from different angles to find the best solution.

I haven't always been this flexible. I used to not be able to see more than one solution to a problem.

For example, I've always used the "bunny rabbit ears" way to tie my shoes. When my friend, Adaptable Ninja, tried to teach me a new way, I just couldn't understand that another way was possible! That's when I knew I had to work on my flexible thinking skills.

It wasn't until Adaptable Ninja showed me the 3 Ts method that I became more flexible in my thinking.

Would you like to know how to be a more flexible thinker, too?
Come on, I'll show you!

The 3 Ts stand for:

- TRY
- TELL
- THINK

Try making new rules for games.
Tell jokes that play with the meanings and sounds of words.
Think out loud about all the possible solutions to a problem.

The first T is to try making new rules for games. Switching up a regular game like Chutes and Ladders can develop our flexible thinking skills.

Instead of climbing up the ladders and sliding down the chutes, we can agree to slide down the ladders and walk up the chutes.

Here's another example:

We can create a new basketball game where we give points depending on the shot we take.

Can you think of a game that you normally play where you can switch the rules of the game up?

The second T is to tell jokes that play with the meanings and sounds of words. We can learn how one word can have multiple meanings.

Here's an example: Why are fish so smart? Because they live in schools. Here the word, schools, have two different meanings:

1. An institution for education
2. A group

Being humorous is a great way to develop flexible thinking skills. Funny Ninja is great at it!

The 3rd T is to think out loud about new ways of doing things. This helps us see more options so we can find the best solution.

Let's look at a math problem. Make 10.

You might say, "5+5," and you would be right!
But there are many solutions to this problem.

1 + 9

2 + 8

6 + 4

As you can see, flexible thinking skills help us find many solutions to a problem. When we come up with different ways to solve a problem, we can then choose the best answer!

Download your Flexible Thinking Ninja Activity Bundle Kit and beyond the book resources at ninjalifehacks.tv

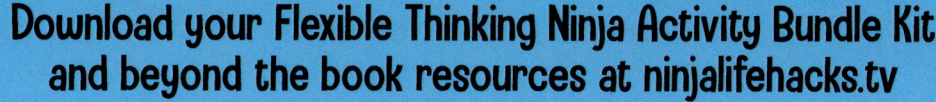
@marynhin   @GrowGrit
#NinjaLifeHacks

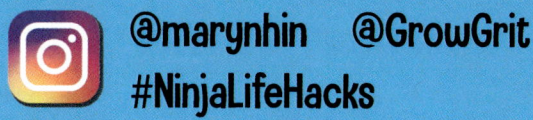
Mary Nhin   Ninja Life Hacks

Ninja Life Hacks

Made in the USA
Monee, IL
13 February 2022